AF515893

Laughs Unlimited: The Big Book of Jokes for Kids

PAYEL CHAKRAVARTY, BTECH (IT), MTECH (IT)

Laughs Unlimited: The Big Book of Jokes for Kids

Mrs. Payel Chakravarty BTech (IT), MTech (IT)

TABLE OF CONTENTS

PREFACE

Welcome to *LAUGHS UNLIMITED: THE BIG BOOK OF JOKES FOR KIDS*!

Laughter is one of the most universal joys in life. It transcends age, culture, and even language. At its heart, a good laugh has the power to bring people together, spark creativity, and lighten even the heaviest of days. This book is a celebration of that power, crafted to deliver countless moments of shared happiness for kids and families alike.

Children are natural comedians. Their curious minds and endless imagination make them uniquely capable of finding humour in the simplest things. This book has been designed to nurture that gift, introducing young readers to a wide range of joke styles—from classic Q&A jokes to mind-bending riddles and tongue twisters. Each chapter is carefully curated to ensure a delightful mix of humour and learning, with jokes that are clean, family-friendly, and truly fun for everyone.

What makes *LAUGHS UNLIMITED* special is its inclusivity. Whether you're an aspiring young comedian, a parent looking for new material to entertain your little ones, or simply someone who loves a good giggle, this book has something for you. With jokes that cover everything from animals and superheroes to schoolyard silliness and seasonal cheer, it promises to keep readers of all ages entertained.

But this book isn't just about telling jokes—it's about creating them, too! In Chapter 12, we encourage young readers to channel their creativity and learn the art of joke-writing. Humour is a skill, and like any skill, it improves with practice. We hope this book inspires kids to explore their own comedic potential, crafting their own punchlines and spreading smiles wherever they go.

At its core, this collection is more than just a compilation of jokes. It's a toolkit for building bonds. Share these jokes with friends during lunch breaks, on long car rides, or around the dinner table. Use them to break the ice, uplift someone's day, or simply enjoy a hearty laugh together. Laughter, after all, is the shortest distance between two people.

We've filled this book with love, care, and plenty of chuckles, hoping it becomes a treasured companion in your home. Whether it's a holiday gathering, a cozy bedtime read, or just a moment of silliness in the middle of the day, *LAUGHS UNLIMITED* is here to deliver endless joy.

So, grab this book, turn the page, and get ready to laugh until your belly hurts. The world of jokes awaits—and it's one you'll want to explore again and again.

Let the laughter begin!
— Mrs. Payel Chakravarty (Author)

INTRODUCTION

What's the one thing that never goes out of style, fits every occasion, and brings people together like magic? Laughter!

Welcome to *Laughs Unlimited: The Big Book of Jokes for Kids*, a treasure chest of giggles, grins, and belly laughs. This book isn't just a collection of jokes; it's an invitation to explore the wonderful world of humour—a world where kids and adults alike can connect through the universal language of laughter.

We all know life can get a little serious at times, but a well-timed joke has the power to brighten even the dullest day. Whether it's a classic knock-knock joke that has everyone chuckling, a tricky riddle that sparks curiosity, or a clever pun that brings out groans and giggles in equal measure, humour is the ultimate icebreaker. And guess what? This book has all that and more!

Why Jokes Matter

Jokes aren't just for fun—they're good for you, too! Studies show that laughter improves mood, strengthens relationships, and even boosts creativity and problem-solving skills. For kids, jokes are a fantastic way to build confidence, sharpen wit, and improve reading and communication skills. Sharing a joke with friends or family can turn an ordinary moment into a special memory, and this book is here to help create countless such moments.

What to Expect

In this book, you'll find a variety of joke styles, themes, and challenges designed to tickle every funny bone:

- **Chapter 2:** Dive into classic Q&A jokes, perfect for quick laughs.

- **Chapter 3:** Discover the timeless fun of knock-knock jokes that never fail to bring a smile.
- **Chapter 4:** Test your brain with riddles that will leave you scratching your head and laughing out loud.
- **Chapters 5–10:** Explore jokes about animals, school, travel, superheroes, seasons, and more—tailored for every interest and occasion.
- **Chapter 11:** Learn fun and quirky facts that will make you laugh while you learn.
- **Chapter 12:** Ready to create your own jokes? This chapter will teach you how to craft setups and punchlines like a pro.

But it doesn't stop there! This book also includes tongue twisters to challenge your speaking skills, bonus one-liners to memorize, and a final chapter filled with the ultimate collection of laughs to leave you smiling for days.

A Book for Everyone

Whether you're a young reader looking for some giggles, a parent hoping to entertain the kids, or someone who simply loves to laugh, this book has been written with you in mind. The jokes are clean, family-friendly, and easy to share. Bring this book to a party, read it on a road trip, or flip through its pages during a quiet evening at home—it's your trusty sidekick for spreading joy wherever you go.

Let's Get Started!

As you turn these pages, you'll find that laughter truly is unlimited. Each joke, riddle, and pun has been selected to ensure you'll always have something new and exciting to share. So, are you ready to become the funniest kid in the room, the ultimate joke-telling champ, or just someone who loves a good laugh?

Grab your favorite snack, call your friends and family, and let the fun begin! With *Laughs Unlimited*, you're not just reading a book—you're stepping into a world of endless joy and boundless laughter.

Let's get laughing!

Chapter 1. Welcome to the World of Jokes!

Hello, gigglers and grin-makers! Welcome to a world where laughter rules, smiles are contagious, and every page is packed with fun! You're about to dive into a joke-tastic adventure that's guaranteed to tickle your funny bone and bring joy to everyone around you. Whether you're here to chuckle, chortle, or laugh until your belly hurts, you've come to the right place.

Why are jokes so special? Well, let me tell you! Jokes are like little pockets of magic—they can brighten your day, turn a frown upside down, and even bring people closer together. Think about it: when you share a joke with your friends or family, everyone starts smiling. Laughter has a way of making moments unforgettable, whether it's a goofy giggle at the dinner table, a roar of laughter on a car ride, or a shared smile at school.

But wait... there's more! Telling jokes isn't just fun; it also makes you super smart. Jokes help you think quickly, come up with clever ideas, and even learn new words. Plus, nothing beats the feeling of making someone else laugh—it's like being a superhero, but instead of saving the day, you're spreading smiles.

So, how about a little warm-up? Here are some quick jokes to get you started:

- Why did the teddy bear skip dessert? Because it was already stuffed!
- What do you call a dinosaur with a great sense of humour? A laugh-a-saurus!

- Why don't skeletons fight each other? They don't have the guts!

Pretty good, right? And there are SO many more where those came from. This book is filled with jokes about animals, food, school, holidays, and just about everything else you can imagine. And the best part? These jokes are meant to be shared! Tell them to your family, your friends, your teachers, or even your pet goldfish. (Though I'm not sure goldfish are known for their sense of humour.)

Remember, laughter isn't just for kids. It's for everyone! So, don't be surprised if the grown-ups around you start laughing harder than you do. Humour has no age limit, and this book is here to prove it.

Alright, enough chit-chat... are you ready to start this laugh-filled adventure? Get those giggles ready and let's turn the page to dive into the funniest world you've ever seen. On your marks, get set, LAUGH!

CHAPTER 2. CLASSIC Q&A JOKES

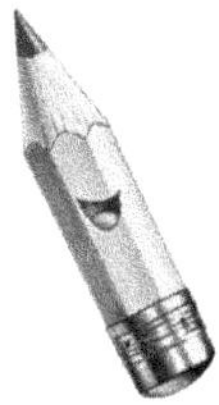

Why did the math book go to therapy?

It had too many problems.

What did the pencil say to the paper?

I'm feeling sharp today!

Why don't skeletons fight each other?

They don't have the guts!

What did one wall say to the other wall?

I'll meet you at the corner!

What's brown and sticky?

A stick!

Why was the broom late?

It swept in!

How do you make a tissue dance?

Put a little boogie in it!

What did the cloud say to the lightning bolt?

You're shocking!

Why do cows wear bells?

Because their horns don't work!

What do you call a sleeping bull?

A bulldozer!

Why did the cookie go to the doctor?

It felt crummy!

How do you organize a space party?

You planet!

Why did the bicycle fall over?

It was two-tired!

What did the grape say when it got stepped on?

Nothing, it just let out a little wine!

Why did the computer go to art school?

To improve its "draw" skills!

Why was the math book sad?

It had too many problems.

What did the fish say when it hit the wall?

Dam!

Why don't eggs tell jokes?

They might crack up!

What did the ocean say to the beach?

Nothing, it just waved!

What do you call a dinosaur with an extensive vocabulary?

A thesaurus!

Why can't you give Elsa a balloon?

Because she'll let it go!

What's a skeleton's least favorite room?

The living room!

What do you call fake noodles?

An impasta!

Why was the computer cold?

It left its Windows open!

Why couldn't the bicycle stand up by itself?

It was two-tired!

How do you catch a squirrel?

Climb up in a tree and act like a nut!

Why do cows make great musicians?

They have good moo-sical taste!

Why don't skeletons ever use cell phones?

They don't have the nerve!

What did the snail say to the turtle?

"Hurry up, slowpoke!"

What do you get when you cross a fish and a piano?

A bass clef!

What did the tree say to the leaf?

"I'm falling for you!"

Why did the scarecrow win an award?
Because he was outstanding in his field!

What did the zero say to the eight? Nice belt!

Why do birds fly south for the winter?

It's faster than walking!

How do you make a tissue dance?

Put a little boogie in it!

Why did the sun go to school?

To get brighter!

What did the banana say to the monkey?

Nothing, bananas can't talk!

What's orange and sounds like a parrot?

A carrot!

Why did the chicken sit on the computer?

To keep an eye on the web!

What's a vampire's favorite fruit?

A necktarine!

What do you get when you cross a snowman and a vampire?

Frostbite!

Why did the skeleton go to the party alone?

He had no body to go with him!

Why don't seagulls fly over the bay?

Because then they'd be called bagels!

What did one hat say to the other?

Stay here, I'm going on ahead!

What kind of tree fits in your hand?

A palm tree!

Why did the bicycle refuse to play cards?

It was afraid of getting a flat tire!

What did the ocean say to the sand?

Nothing, it just waved!

Why don't skeletons ever fight?

They don't have the stomach for it!

How does a penguin build its house?

Igloos it together!

Why did the scarecrow love his job?

He was outstanding in his field!

What do you get when you cross a snowman and a dog?
Frostbite!

Why did the tomato turn red?

Because it saw the salad dressing!

What's a math teacher's favorite place in NYC?

Times Square!

How do you make a fruit punch?

Give it a boxing lesson!

What did the grape do when it got stepped on?

Nothing, it just let out a little wine!

Why did the giraffe get bad grades?

He had his head in the clouds!

Why was the broom late?

It had to sweep through traffic!

Why did the bird get a ticket?

It was caught speeding in a school zone!

What's the longest word in the dictionary?

Smiles, because there's a mile between the first and last letter!

Why don't skeletons fight each other?

They don't have the guts!

What did the paper say to the pencil?

"I'm feeling sharp!"

How do you make holy water?

You boil the hell out of it!

Why did the tomato go to the party?

Because it was a little saucy!

How do cows stay in touch?

They moo-mail!

Why did the computer keep sneezing?

It had a virus!

Why was the computer so good at school?

It had a lot of bytes!

What do you call a bear with no teeth?

A gummy bear!

How do you organize a party in space?

You planet!

What do you call a fish who practices medicine?

A sturgeon!

What's brown and sounds like a bell?

Dung!

Why do elephants never use computers?

They're afraid of the mouse!

Why don't skeletons ever go out in the snow?

They're afraid they'll get cold feet!

Why did the bicycle fall over?

It was two-tired!

Why was the calendar so popular?

It had a lot of dates!

Why did the pencil go to school?

It used the mashed potatoes!

What did the balloon say to the pin?

You're about to pop my bubble!

Why did the bicycle refuse to play cards?

It was afraid of getting a flat tire!

To get a little lead-ership!

How did the cow become a movie star?

It was always moo-ving the camera!

Why was the math book sad?

It had too many problems!

What do you get when you cross a fish and an elephant?

Swimming trunks!

What's orange and sounds like a parrot?

A carrot!

What did one shoe say to the other?

"You're the sole mate!"

What kind of music do balloons hate?

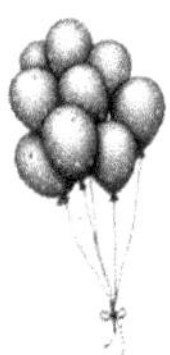

Pop!

How do you make holy water?

You boil the hell out of it!

Why was the broom late?

It swept in!

What do you call a fish with no eyes?

Fsh!

Why don't skeletons fight each other?

They don't have the stomach for it!

Why don't skeletons use cell phones?

They don't have the nerve!

What did the sandwich say to the bread?

You're the best thing since sliced bread!

What's a vampire's favourite fruit?

A necktarine!

What did the apple say to the orange?

You're a-peeling!

Why did the duck get a pen?

To draw some quackers!

Why was the dog a great musician?

It had perfect "paws-ition!"

What do you call a snake who works for the government?

A civil serpent!

Why did the bicycle go to the party?

It wanted to "wheel" in the fun!

What did the snowman say to the carrot?

"You're the pick of the patch!"

Why did the chicken cross the road?

To get to the other side!

What's a skeleton's least favourite room?

The living room!

Why did the coffee file a police report?

It got mugged!

What did one plate say to the other?

Lunch is on me!

Why did the apple stop in the middle of the road?

It ran out of juice!

How do cows stay in touch?

They moo-mail!

What did the cactus say to the flower?

"You've got a blooming good attitude!"

What do you call a chicken who's good at math?

A math-a-saurus!

Why was the book so unhappy?

Because it had too many pages to turn!

What did one pencil say to the other pencil?

"You're looking sharp!"

What do you call an alligator in a vest?

An investigator!

Why did the orange stop?

It ran out of juice!

What did the snail say to the turtle?

"Hurry up, slowpoke!"

What did the grape do when it got stepped on?

Nothing, it just let out a little wine!

Why did the dog sit in the shade?

It didn't want to be a hot dog!

How do you organize a space party?

You planet!

What did the snowman wear to the party?

An ice-cold smile!

Why was the calendar so popular?

It had a lot of dates!

What did one lamp say to the other lamp?

"You light up my life!"

Why did the bicycle break up with the unicycle?

It wanted more stability!

What did the lightning bolt say to the thunder?

"You're so loud!"

Why did the ghost refuse to go to the party?

He had no body to go with!

Why did the chicken join the band?

Because it had the drumsticks!

How does a snowman get around?

By riding an "icicle"!

What did the pasta say to the sauce?

"You complete me!"

What's the best way to make a tissue dance?

Put a little boogie in it!

What did the strawberry say to the banana?

"You're a-peeling!"

How do cows stay in touch?

With Moo-mail!

What did the zero say to the eight?

Nice belt!

Why did the giraffe get a promotion?

Because he was outstanding in his field!

Why did the fish blush?

It saw the ocean's bottom!

What do you call a ghost who tells jokes?

A pun-isher!

How do you stop a dog from barking in your car?

Take the dog out of the car!

What did the grape say to the banana?

"Stop peeling around!"

Why was the dog sitting on the math book?

It wanted to be a "puppy" mathematician!

What do you call a fake noodle?

An impasta!

Why did the snowman call for a taxi?

He wanted a "snowmobile" ride!

How did the pencil feel after it was sharpened?

It felt "pointed" in the right direction!

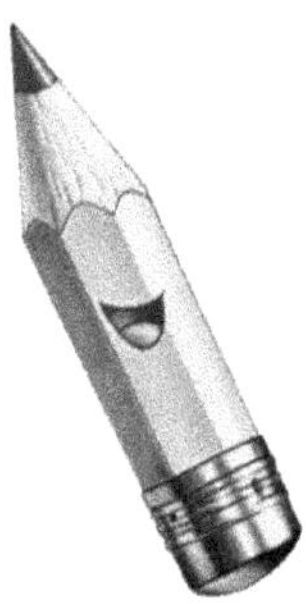

Why did the bicycle fall over?

It was two-tired!

Why don't skeletons use cell phones?

They don't have the nerve!

What did the skeleton say to the vampire?

"You're looking fang-tastic!"

Why was the grape always smiling?

Because it couldn't stop "wine-ing"!

What did the cat say to the dog?

"Stop barking at me, I'm feline good!"

Why did the scarecrow win an award?

Because he was outstanding in his field!

What did one pencil say to the other pencil?

"You're looking sharp!"

Why don't skeletons fight each other?

They don't have the stomach for it!

What did one cow say to the other cow?

"Move over, I need some space!"

Why was the math book sad?

It had too many problems!

What's orange and sounds like a parrot?

A carrot!

How do you make a fruit punch?

Give it a boxing lesson!

What did the fish say when it hit the wall?

Dam!

Why did the bicycle go to school?

To get "wheeled" away!

What's the best way to organize a space party?

You planet!

Why was the football team always in trouble?

They kept getting caught "kicking" around!

How do you organize a space party?

You planet!

What did the volcano say to the earthquake?

"You rock my world!"

How do you fix a broken pencil?

Use a "lead" patch!

Why did the dog sit in the shade?

Because it didn't want to be a hot dog!

How do you organize a party in space?

You planet!

What did one donut say to the other?

"I'm feeling dough-lightful today!"

What did the cucumber say to the tomato?

"You're looking vine-ripened!"

Why was the notebook always calm?

Because it knew how to keep its pages in order!

What do you get when you cross a snowman with a vampire?

Frostbite!

Why was the broom always late?

It swept in!

What did the cloud say to the lightning bolt?

"You're shocking!"

What do you call a bird who loves math?

A "counting" bird!

What did the pencil say to the eraser?

"I'm not worried, you'll erase my mistakes!"

What did the cat say to the fish?

"I'm hooked on you!"

How do you make holy water?

Boil the hell out of it!

What did one calendar say to the other?

"You're getting all booked up!"

What did the snowman wear to the party?

An ice-cold smile!

Why did the chair go to school?

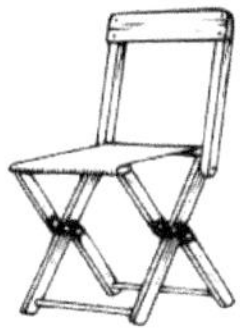

To get its seat in class!

What did the ocean say to the boat?

Nothing, it just waved!

How do you organize a space party?

You planet!

What did the skeleton use to cross the street?

A "bone"-fied crosswalk!

What do you call a train full of bubble gum?

A chew-chew train!

What did one hat say to the other?

"Stay here, I'm going on ahead!"

Why was the skeleton always on time?

He had a bone to pick!

What do you call a fish that practices medicine?

A sturgeon!

Why did the elephant bring a suitcase?

Because it wanted to pack its trunk!

What did one clock say to the other clock?

"It's time to meet up!"

Why did the giraffe get bad grades?

He had his head in the clouds!

Why was the math teacher so popular?

Because she had all the right "angles!"

What did the dog say to the bone?

"You're my chew-mate!"

How did the bird get its promotion?

By working on its "tweeting" skills!

Why did the grape never get lonely?

It had a bunch of friends!

Why was the chair a great comedian?

It had a lot of "sit-com" material!

How do cows stay in touch?

Moo-mail!

Why was the fish always the last one picked?

Because it was always "fin-ishing" last!

What did the apple say to the banana?

"You're a-peeling!"

Why did the apple stop?

It ran out of juice!

What did the tree say to the leaf?

"I'm falling for you!"

Why do cows wear bells?

Because their horns don't work!

How does a snowman get around?

By riding an "icicle!"

Why did the bicycle go to the beach?

To "wheel" in the fun!

CHAPTER 3. KNOCK-KNOCK FUN

Knock, knock!

Who's there?

Cows go.

Cows go who?

No, silly—cows go "moo"!

Knock, knock!

Who's there?

Dishes.

Dishes who?

Dishes the funniest joke ever!

Knock, knock!

Who's there?

Gorilla.

Gorilla who?

Gorilla me a burger, I'm starving!

Knock, knock!

Who's there?

Ash.

Ash who?

Ash you a question—do you like knock-knock jokes?

Knock, knock!

Who's there?

Olive.

Olive who?

Olive having fun—how about you?

Knock, knock!

Who's there?

Tuba.

Tuba who?

Tuba toothpaste is better than one!

Knock, knock!

Who's there?

Cargo.

Cargo who?

Cargo beep beep—vroom vroom!

Knock, knock!

Who's there?

Wooden.

Wooden who?

Wooden you like to hear another joke?

Knock, knock!

Who's there?

Ice cream.

Ice cream who?

Ice cream every time I hear a funny joke!

Knock, knock!

Who's there?

Leaf.

Leaf who?

Leaf the door open—I'm coming in!

Knock, knock!

Who's there?

Cow.

Cow who?

Cow me in—I love jokes!

Knock, knock!

Who's there?

Lettuce.

Lettuce who?

Lettuce laugh together—it's fun!

Knock, knock!

Who's there?

Pencil.

Pencil who?

Pencil be your new favorite joke!

Knock, knock!

Who's there?

Atch.

Atch who?

Bless you!

Knock, knock!

Who's there?

Water.

Water who?

Water you doing? Open the door!

Knock, knock!

Who's there?

Cheddar.

Cheddar who?

Cheddar late than never!

Knock, knock!

Who's there?

Nacho.

Nacho who?

Nacho cheese—it's mine!

Knock, knock!

Who's there?

Dough.

Dough who?

Doughnut forget to smile!

Knock, knock!

Who's there?

Boo.

Boo who?

Boo-tiful day for a joke, isn't it?

Knock, knock!

Who's there?

Bear.

Bear who?

Bear-ly hanging on for another laugh!

Knock, knock!

Who's there?

Chicken.

Chicken who?

Chicken out my new dance moves!

Knock, knock!

Who's there?

Alpaca.

Alpaca who?

Alpaca the suitcase for our trip!

Knock, knock!

Who's there?

Broccoli.

Broccoli who?

Broccoli your jokes are the best!

Knock, knock!

Who's there?

Snow.

Snow who?

Snow use pretending you don't love jokes!

Knock, knock!

Who's there?

Butter.

Butter who?

Butter open the door—I'm here!

Knock, knock!

Who's there?

Candy.

Candy who?

Candy you believe how funny this is?

Knock, knock!

Who's there?

Turnip.

Turnip who?

Turnip the music—it's party time!

Knock, knock!

Who's there?

Peas.

Peas who?

Peas open the door!

Knock, knock!

Who's there?

Fig.

Fig who?

Fig-ure out who it is yet?

Knock, knock!

Who's there?

Olive.

Olive who?

Olive you and I mean it!

Knock, knock!

Who's there?

T-Rex.

T-Rex who?

T-Rex your door—it's broken now!

Knock, knock!

Who's there?

Kiwi.

Kiwi who?

Kiwi be friends?

Knock, knock!

Who's there?

Popcorn.

Popcorn who?

Popcorn and open the door!

Knock, knock!

Who's there?

Raisin.

Raisin who?

Raisin a toast to all these jokes!

Knock, knock!

Who's there?

Toast.

Toast who?

Toast-ally me knocking!

Knock, knock!

Who's there?

Ham.

Ham who?

Ham-burger is my favorite food!

Knock, knock!

Who's there?

Bee.

Bee who?

Bee ready for the funniest joke yet!

Knock, knock!

Who's there?

Balloon.

Balloon who?

Balloon up the room with laughter!

Knock, knock!

Who's there?

Berry.

Berry who?

Berry nice to meet you!

Knock, knock!

Who's there?

Anchor.

Anchor who?

Anchor you going to let me in?

Knock, knock!

Who's there?

Cheese.

Cheese who?

Cheese the funniest knock-knock jokes ever!

Knock, knock!

Who's there?

Fish.

Fish who?

Fish you'd laugh at my jokes more!

Knock, knock!

Who's there?

Shark.

Shark who?

Shark-tastic to see you!

Knock, knock!

Who's there?

Plant.

Plant who?

Plant your feet—I've got more jokes!

Knock, knock!

Who's there?

Donkey.

Donkey who?

Donkey laugh too hard—you'll fall!

Knock, knock!

Who's there?

Goat.

Goat who?

Goat to open the door—it's me!

Knock, knock!

Who's there?

Corn.

Corn who?

Corn-gratulations, you love this joke!

Knock, knock!

Who's there?

Penguin.

Penguin who?

Penguin you going to let me in?

Knock, knock!

Who's there?

Apple.

Apple who?

Apple-lause for all these jokes!

Knock, knock!

Who's there?

Piano.

Piano who?

Piano-t you glad I knocked?

Knock, knock!

Who's there?

Alpaca.

Alpaca who?

Alpaca suitcase for the trip—are you ready?

Knock, knock!

Who's there?

Egg.

Egg who?

Egg-cited to crack you up!

Knock, knock!

Who's there?

Tank.

Tank who?

You're welcome!

Knock, knock!

Who's there?

Broccoli.

Broccoli who?

Broccoli your doorbell isn't working!

Knock, knock!

Who's there?

Butter.

Butter who?

Butter open the door—it's me!

Knock, knock!

Who's there?

Mirror.

Mirror who?

Mirror-ly here to make you laugh!

Knock, knock!

Who's there?

Jellybean.

Jellybean who?

Jellybean waiting for you to answer!

Knock, knock!

Who's there?

Bicycle.

Bicycle who?

Bicycle you later—gotta ride off!

Knock, knock!

Who's there?

Ninja.

Ninja who?

Ninja worry, I'm here with jokes!

Knock, knock!

Who's there?

Robot.

Robot who?

Robot you didn't know I was funny?

Knock, knock!

Who's there?

Fudge.

Fudge who?

Fudge-ment day is here—it's joke time!

Knock, knock!

Who's there?

Snail.

Snail who?

Snail I see you again soon?

Knock, knock!

Who's there?

Paper.

Paper who?

Paper airplane—it's flying to your door!

Knock, knock!

Who's there?

Cupcake.

Cupcake who?

Cupcake and see me later!

Knock, knock!

Who's there?

Whale.

Whale who?

Whale, hello there!

Knock, knock!

Who's there?

Toast.

Toast who?

Toast to a day full of laughs!

Knock, knock!

Who's there?

Pickle.

Pickle who?

Pickle me a better joke, I dare you!

Knock, knock!

Who's there?

Sprinkle.

Sprinkle who?

Sprinkle a little laughter in your life!

Knock, knock!

Who's there?

Kangaroo.

Kangaroo who?

Kangaroo believe how funny I am?

Knock, knock!

Who's there?

Cereal.

Cereal who?

Cereal-sly, open the door!

Knock, knock!

Who's there?

Button.

Button who?

Button up, it's cold out here!

Knock, knock!

Who's there?

Anchor.

Anchor who?

Anchor you glad I stopped by?

Knock, knock!

Who's there?

Nacho.

Nacho who?

Nacho average joke-teller!

Knock, knock!

Who's there?

Zipper.

Zipper who?

Zipper-dee-doo-dah, I'm here!

Knock, knock!

Who's there?

Mushroom.

Mushroom who?

Mushroom for one more joke?

Knock, knock!

Who's there?

Tractor.

Tractor who?

Tractor your laughter—it's missing!

Knock, knock!

Who's there?

Penguin.

Penguin who?

Penguin you going to open the door?

Knock, knock!

Who's there?

Star.

Star who?

Star you going to laugh or what?

Knock, knock!

Who's there?

Puddle.

Puddle who?

Puddle down, it's just me!

Knock, knock!

Who's there?

Glitter.

Glitter who?

Glitter laugh out loud—these are great!

Knock, knock!

Who's there?

Napkin.

Napkin who?

Napkin you give me a smile?

Knock, knock!

Who's there?

Pilot.

Pilot who?

Pilot up the laughter—it's flying high!

Knock, knock!

Who's there?

Crayon.

Crayon who?

Crayon you let me in already?

Knock, knock!

Who's there?

Cup.

Cup who?

Cup-lifting jokes, right?

Knock, knock!

Who's there?

Sauce.

Sauce who?

Sauce you soon—it's joke time!

Knock, knock!

Who's there?

Wrapper.

Wrapper who?

Wrapper you ready for another?

Knock, knock!

Who's there?

Balloon.

Balloon who?

Balloon up some more laughter, will ya?

Knock, knock!

Who's there?

Feather.

Feather who?

Feather or not you're laughing, I'm here!

Knock, knock!

Who's there?

Toolbox.

Toolbox who?

Toolbox full of jokes—want one?

Knock, knock!

Who's there?

Snowflake.

Snowflake who?

Snowflake me laugh like that again!

Knock, knock!

Who's there?

Pogo.

Pogo who?

Pogo stick with me, I've got more!

Knock, knock!

Who's there?

Fishy.

Fishy who?

Fishy you'd open the door faster!

Knock, knock!

Who's there?

Jelly.

Jelly who?

Jelly me another joke—it's fun!

Knock, knock!

Who's there?

Slide.

Slide who?

Slide over and let me in!

Knock, knock!

Who's there?

Lemon.

Lemon who?

Lemon you in on a little secret—it's a joke!

Knock, knock!

Who's there?

Anchor.

Anchor who?

Anchor we going to keep joking forever?

Knock, knock!

Who's there?

Moose.

Moose who?

Moose you laugh more at my jokes?

Knock, knock!

Who's there?

Book.

Book who?

Book it—I'm on the best joke list now!.

CHAPTER 4. RIDDLE ME THIS!

What has hands but can't clap?

A clock!

What can you catch but not throw?

A cold!

What has a face, two arms, but no legs?

A clock!

What gets wetter the more it dries?

A towel!

What has a neck but no head?

A bottle!

What has one eye but can't see?

A needle!

What is full of holes but still holds water?

A sponge!

What has keys but can't open doors?

A piano!

What comes down but never goes up?

Rain!

What gets sharper the more you use it but isn't a knife?

Your brain!

What has a heart that doesn't beat?

An artichoke!

What has a bed but never sleeps?

A river!

What has no wings but can still fly?

A kite!

What has ears but can't hear?

Corn!

What can you hold in your right hand but never in your left?

Your left hand!

What has a tail and a head but no body?

A coin!

What has four wheels and flies?

A garbage truck!

What goes up but never comes down?

Your age!

What has words but never speaks?

A book!

What's as light as a feather but even the strongest person can't hold it for long?

Your breath!

What has stripes but never roars?

A zebra crossing!

What's orange and sounds like a parrot?

A carrot!

What has roots but never grows?

A family tree!

What has a thumb and four fingers but isn't alive?

A glove!

What do you call cheese that isn't yours?

Nacho cheese!

What has a bottom at the top?

Your legs!

What kind of tree can you hold in your hand?

A palm tree!

What's always in front of you but can't be seen?

The future!

What has a head, a tail, but no body?

A coin!

What runs but never walks?

A faucet!

What has a bark but no bite?

A tree!

What's black and white and read all over?

A newspaper!

What's bigger when it's upside down?

The number 6!

What has eyes but can't see?

A potato!

What has a ring but no finger?

A telephone!

What comes in two but can never be separated?

Scissors!

What goes around the world but stays in the same spot?

A stamp!

What's always moving but stays in one place?

A clock!

What starts with T, ends with T, and is filled with T?

A teapot!

What has cities but no houses, forests but no trees, rivers but no water?

A map!

What has teeth but doesn't eat?

A comb!

What's so fragile that saying its name breaks it?

Silence!

What has legs but doesn't walk?

A table!

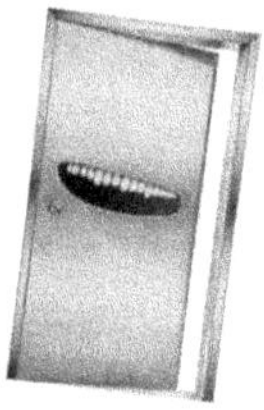

What has a handle but no lid?

A door!

What has a horn but doesn't honk?

A unicorn!

What's blue, has fins, and likes to write?

A ballpoint fish!

What's round, orange, and sounds like a bell?

A ding-orange!

What do you call a bear with no teeth?

A gummy bear!

What has stripes but isn't a tiger?

A candy cane!

What flies around all day but never lands?

Time!

What has buttons but no holes?

A remote control!

What has a spine but no bones?

A book!

What kind of room has no doors or windows?

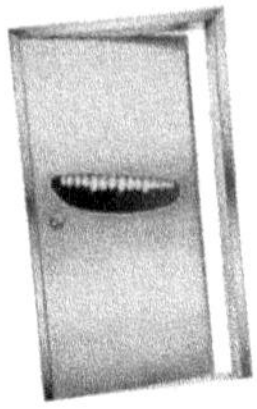

A mushroom!

What can travel around the world while staying in the corner?

A stamp!

What can you throw but never catch?

A tantrum!

What has wheels but isn't a car?

A shopping cart!

What's red, round, and has seeds but isn't a watermelon?

A tomato!

What starts out on four legs, moves to two legs, and then three legs?

A person (crawling, walking, using a cane)!

What has a tongue but never talks?

A shoe!

What's white, fluffy, and comes out of the sky?

Snow!

What gets bigger the more you take away from it?

A hole!

What can fill a room but takes up no space?

Light!

What can you serve but never eat?

A tennis ball!

What has feathers but doesn't fly?

A feather duster!

What's shaped like a donut but you can't eat?

A life preserver!

What has a ring but you can't wear?

A doorbell!

What can go up a chimney down but not down a chimney up?

An umbrella!

What's small, green, and runs as fast as lightning?

A grasshopper!

What has stripes but isn't on a zebra?

A barcode!

What has a head, a foot, and four legs but isn't alive?

A bed!

What comes out at night without being called?

The stars!

What do you call a cat on a computer?

A mouse chaser!

What has feathers and tells time?

A cuckoo clock!

What can you break but never touch?

A promise!

What gets lost every time it's spoken?

A secret!

What's sweet, sticky, and comes from bees?

Honey!

What has paws but doesn't walk?

A teddy bear!

What has four eyes but can't see?

Mississippi!

What has two heads, six legs, and a tail?

A person riding a horse!

What grows the more you take away from it?

A subtraction problem!

What comes up but never goes down?

The sun in the morning!

What's as big as an elephant but weighs nothing?

Its shadow!

What has wings but can't fly?

A penguin!

What do you get when you cross a snowman and a dog?

Frostbite!

What goes tick-tock but doesn't tell time?

A metronome!

What's the fastest vegetable in the garden?

A runner bean!

What's green and can be caught but never held?

A frog's leap!

What has a sound but no mouth?

An echo!

What kind of tree fits in your hand?

A palm tree!

What's white and has a black spot but isn't a Dalmatian?

A domino!

What jumps when it walks and sits when it stands?

A kangaroo!

What's yellow, has a peel, but isn't a banana?

A lemon!

What has teeth but never eats?

A zipper!

What has numbers but isn't a clock?

A calendar!

What's fluffy, white, and comes in the sky?

A cloud!

What has a roof but no walls?

A car!

What's blue, wet, and covers most of the Earth?

The ocean!

What has four legs, two arms, and says "ribbit"?

A frog prince!

What's the best tool for telling time?

A sundial!

What's sweet, yellow, and good at math?

A lemon-aid stand!

CHAPTER 5. ANIMAL ANTICS

Why did the zebra always get invited to the party?

Because it knew how to stripe up a good time!

What's a lion's favorite fast food?

A cheetah burger!

Why did the cat sit on the computer?

To keep an eye on the mouse!

What do you get when you cross a shark and a snowman?

Frostbite!

What did the horse say when it fell down?

"I've hoof got to get up!"

Why don't squirrels ever share their acorns?

Because they're a little nutty!

What did the whale say to the shrimp?

Stop being so shellfish!

Why did the owl become a comedian?

Because it was great at hooting up laughs!

What do you call a rabbit with a bad haircut?

A hare-cut disaster!

Why did the cow go to space?

To see the mooon!

What do you call a dog magician?

A labra-cadabra-dor!

What do you call a fish who loves playing basketball?

A slam-fish!

Why did the turtle wear a backpack?

Because it was going on a shell trip!

What's a crocodile's favorite candy?

Gummy snakes!

What did the duck say to the waiter?

"Put it on my bill!"

What do you get when you cross a goat and a computer?

A byte of the future!

Why don't ants play cards?

Because they're always anticipating the next move!

Why did the cat bring a pencil to the party?

Because it wanted to draw attention!

What do you call an alligator in a vest?

An investigator!

What do you get when you cross a dinosaur and a pig?

A Jurassic Pork!

Why did the cow go on a diet?

Because it wanted to stay moo-tivated!

What's a giraffe's favorite type of music?

Neck-and-roll!

Why did the frog take the bus to work?

Because his car got toad away!

What do you call a snake that's 3.14 meters long?

A pi-thon!

Why do horses always look so calm?

Because they're always in stable conditions!

What's a bear's favorite ice cream?

Brrr-y!

Why do flamingos make terrible baseball players?

Because they can't stand up to the pressure!

What do you call a penguin in the desert?

Lost!

Why did the dog sit in the shade?

Because it didn't want to be a hot dog!

What did the lion say to the tiger at lunch?

"You purrfectly know how to share!"

Why did the dog bring a pencil to the party?

Because he wanted to draw some pawsitive attention!

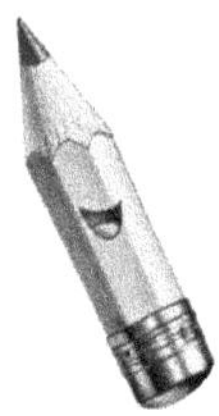

What did the cat say when it saw the empty food bowl?

"This is purr-fectly unacceptable!"

What's a sheep's favorite sport?

Woolleyball!

What do you call a giraffe with no spots?

A plain giraffe!

Why did the snake refuse to play cards?

Because he was afraid of the deck!

What do you get when you cross a dog and a computer?

A retriever!

Why do chickens never tell secrets?

Because they egg each other on!

Why did the cat join Instagram?

To get more furr-ends!

What do you get when you cross an elephant and a rhinoceros?

An ell-ifino!

Why do cows make terrible comedians?

Because their jokes are always moo-ving at a slow pace!

Why did the raccoon break up with his girlfriend?

Because she was too much of a trash talker!

What do you get when you cross a lion and a tiger?

A liger – it's a real roar to handle!

Why did the chicken start a band?

Because it had the drumsticks!

What did the koala say to the tree?

"I'm koalafied to hang out here!"

What do you call a rabbit who wears a tuxedo?

A dapper hare!

Why was the spider such a good baseball player?

Because it had a web of skills!

What do you call a cow on a trampoline?

A milkshake!

Why don't leopards ever play hide-and-seek?

Because they're always spotted!

What do you call a fish who loves to share?

A school fish!

Why did the lion eat the comedian?

He wanted to enjoy some roaring humor!

Why did the owl join the music band?

Because it was great at hoots and notes!

What do you get when you cross a dog with a phone?

A golden receiver!

Why did the horse always make bad jokes?

Because it had no neighboring sense of humor!

What do you call a penguin in a tuxedo?

A formal fowl!

Why don't cows ever win at poker?

Because they always moove their cards around!

What did the elephant say when it saw a mouse?

"Squeak to you later!"

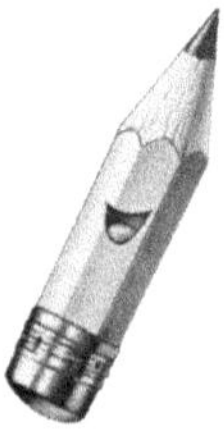

Why did the rabbit bring a pencil to school?

Because it wanted to hare its ideas!

What's a dog's favorite instrument?

The trom-bone!

Why did the giraffe get in trouble at school?

Because it was always necking the answers!

What do you call a snake that likes to play poker?

A card-iac!

Why did the bird join a gym?

To get a tweet body!

What's an alligator's favorite type of music?

Snap!

Why did the mouse bring a suitcase to the party?

Because it was ready to cheese the day!

What do you get when you cross a dog and a snowman?

Frostbite!

Why did the cow get an award?

Because it was outstanding in its field!

What do you call a bear caught in the rain?

A drizzly bear!

Why did the chicken sit at the computer?

Because it wanted to keep an eye on the web!

What's a crab's favorite restaurant?

The Seafood Grill!

Why did the dolphin bring a towel to the beach?

Because it was ready to splash around!

What do you call a sheep that tells jokes?

A baa-d comedian!

What did the cat say to the dog?

"You're paws-itively barking mad!"

Why did the tortoise refuse to race the hare?

Because he was already shell-shocked from the last one!

What did the tiger wear to the party?

A stripes suit!

What do you get when you cross an elephant with a rhinoceros?

An ell-ifino!

Why did the fish blush?

Because it saw the ocean's bottom!

What do you call an animal that's always on time?

A punctu-al bear!

Why did the lion eat the comedian?

It wanted to enjoy some roaring humor!

What do you call a dog who loves to play basketball?

A slam-dunk dog!

What do you call a dragon who loves music?

A rock-and-roll dragon!

What do you call a cat who becomes a detective?

A purr-ivate investigator!

Why do horses make terrible comedians?

Because their jokes are too stable!

What's a dog's favorite snack?

A bark bar!

Why don't flamingos play soccer?

Because they're too leggy!

What do you call a snake who's a detective?

A hiss-tory expert!

Why don't elephants ever make good pilots?

Because they have trouble with trunks!

What did the rabbit say when it got a job offer?

"I'm hare to help!"

What did the wolf say to the sheep at the party?

"You're looking baaa-rilliant tonight!"

Why did the kangaroo join a gym?

To get its jump in shape!

What's a cat's favorite subject in school?

Purrfect geometry!

Why did the crocodile start a band?

Because it wanted to make some snappy music!

What do you call a cat that likes to eat lemons?

A sour puss!

Why did the squirrel bring a pencil to school?

Because it wanted to draw acorns!

What do you call an animal who loves parties?

A wild party animal!

What's a giraffe's favorite drink?

Necktar!

What do you call a kangaroo with a trampoline?

A jumping jack!

Why did the fish hate sharing?

Because it was shellfish!

What did the owl say after telling a joke?

"Hoo's laughing now?"

What do you call a snake that works at a bakery?

A python roll!

What did the dog say to the bone?

"*You're paws-itively awesome!"

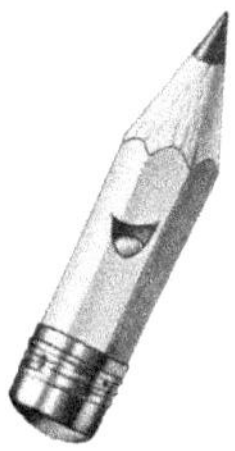

Why did the horse eat a pencil?

Because it wanted to draw some mane ideas!.

CHAPTER 6. SCHOOLYARD LAUGHS

Why did the teacher wear sunglasses?

Because her students were so bright!

Why was the math book so sad?

Because it had too many problems!

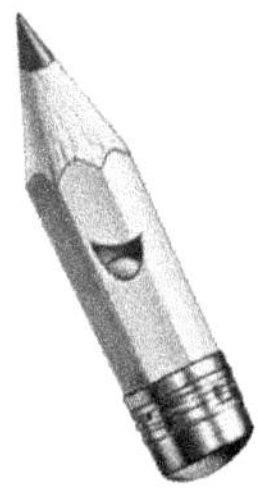

What did one pencil say to the other pencil?

You're sharp!

Why did the student bring a ladder to school?

Because they wanted to go to high school!

What's a math teacher's favorite place in the beach?

The summer!

Why did the computer go to school?

To improve its web-sight!

What do you call a class full of students who love to dance?

A break dance class!

Why don't skeletons fight each other in school?

They don't have the guts!

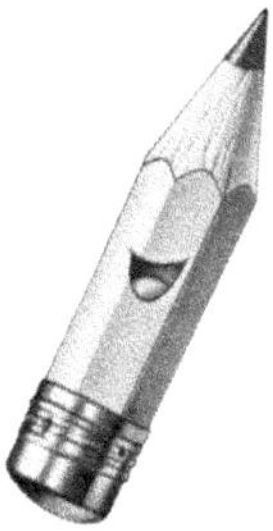

Why was the pencil so afraid?

It was about to be sharpened for a test!

What did the student say to the pencil?

You're so pointed!

Why was the history book so tired?

It had too many pages to turn!

What's the best way to make a tissue dance?

Put a little boogey in it!

Why did the student eat his homework?

Because the teacher said it was a piece of cake!

What did the science teacher say to the student who was acting out?

You're causing a reaction!

Why did the geography book look so nervous?

Because it was always going around the world!

What did the gym teacher do when they couldn't find the ball?

They bounced back!

Why don't school lockers ever tell secrets?

Because they're always locked up tight!

You need to study a little harder!

Why can't you trust math teachers?

Because they're always trying to figure things out!

Why was the computer so good at math?

It had a lot of byte!

What did the class clown bring to school?

A joke notebook!

Why was the librarian always so calm?

Because she was always booked for the day!

What's a school's favorite type of music?

Pop quiz!

Why did the student bring a pencil to art class?

Because it was sketching for inspiration!

What did the teacher say to the student who failed the test?

Why did the class pet hamster fail math?

Because he was always running out of time!

What did the student say to the new lunch lady?

"I think you're grate!"

Why don't eggs ever show up late to school?

Because they're always eggcellent at being on time!

What did the teacher say when the student asked for help with a project?

I'm here to assist you all the way!

Why did the class go to the ocean for the field trip?

To learn how to wave at the fish!

What do you call a class that loves to sing?

A chorus class!

Why don't you ever ask a clock to do your homework?

Because it's always ticking!

Why did the student bring a broom to school?

To sweep through the tests!

What do you call a class full of monkeys?

A banana study session!

What did one wall say to the other wall?

I'll meet you at the corner!

What's a math teacher's favorite type of tree?

A fig tree!

Why do calculators never get in trouble at school?

Because they're always counting on the teacher!

Why did the pencil break up with the paper?

Because it couldn't draw any conclusions!

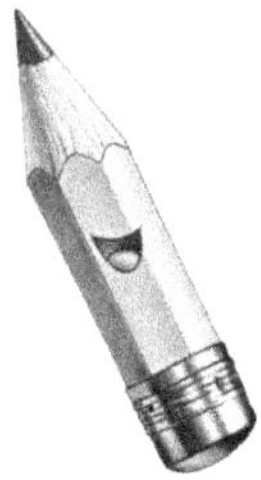

What did the teacher say to the student who was always tired?

You need to rest your mind!

What's a ghost's favorite subject in school?

Spirited away to history class!

Why was the student so good at geography?

Because he knew all the landmarks!

What did the homework say to the student?

"You're not getting rid of me that easily!"

What's the hardest part about school for an astronaut?

Getting past the space tests!

What did the teacher say after giving a pop quiz?

Get ready to ace it!

Why did the student always get in trouble during lunchtime?

Because he was chewing on his words!

What do you call a school for reptiles?

A snakes and learn school!

What did the class say when they saw the homework?

"Not again! We've got work to do!"

Why don't pencils ever argue with pens?

Because they're always pointed in different directions!

What do you get when you mix school with a joke?

A punderful lesson!

Why was the art student so tired?

Because they had a sketchy night!

What did the music teacher say to the student who was playing off-key?

"You need to tune up!"

Why did the student put his homework in the freezer?

Because he wanted to chill before doing it!

What do you call a student who loves to color?

A crayon enthusiast!

Why don't school lockers ever get lost?

Because they always stay in their place!

What did the teacher do when the student dropped a pencil?

She said, "That's pointed behavior!"

Why did the teacher go to the beach?

To school the waves!

What do you call a lazy math student?

A slacker!

Why do frogs do so well in school?

Because they're always jumping to conclusions!

What did the notebook say to the pencil?

"Stop writing me off!"

Why was the library so quiet?

Because everyone was booked for the day!

Why did the teacher break up with the calculator?

Because it wasn't adding anything to her life!

What did the teacher say to the student who couldn't stop talking?

"Let's take a break from your chat!"

What do you call a musical teacher who loves to play jokes?

A note-worthy comedian!

Why don't schools let ghosts enroll?

Because they vanish before they finish their homework!

What do you call a math class in space?

Planet geometry!

Why did the book join the school play?

It wanted to be written into the script!

Why don’t shoes ever do well in school?

Because they always flip out!

What did the music teacher say to the out-of-tune violin player?

"That’s off-key behavior!"

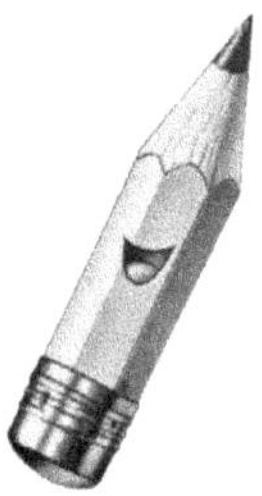

Why did the pencil always feel special in class?

Because it was always pointed in the right direction!

What’s the most organized subject at school?

History! It always has great timelines!

What do you call a bee who loves school?

A buzzing student!

Why did the student carry a pencil sharpener to school?

Because they wanted to keep their thoughts sharp!

Why was the teacher so good at arithmetic?

Because she had countless ways to solve problems!

What's a dog's least favorite subject at school?

Barking language!

What do you call a student who's always organizing the papers?

A file genius!

Why did the computer fail the test?

It had too many bytes to study!

Why did the student bring a ruler to lunch?

To measure their sandwich!

What do you call a fast student?

A speed learner!

Why did the chalk break up with the board?

It felt like it was being erased from the relationship!

Why did the scissors get a detention?

Because it was always cutting in line!

What's the teacher's favourite type of candy?

Smarties!

Why was the teacher always calm during tests?

Because they had all the answers!

What do you call a sleepy student?

A snoozer in class!

Why did the math student bring a flashlight?

Because they wanted to shed light on the problem!

Why did the eraser feel left out?

Because it always came last in the line-up!

What do you get when you cross a school bus and a balloon?

A ride that's full of airy ideas!

Why did the student sit under the desk?

They wanted to study in low-pressure conditions!

Why was the whiteboard so confident?

Because it had a clean slate every day!

What do you call a class full of bees?

The buzzing brigade!

Why did the student take their art project to the doctor?

Because it looked a little sketchy!

Why did the clock join the debate team?

It wanted to make its point!

What's a cat's favorite subject in school?

Hiss-tory!

Why did the stapler go to the principal's office?

Because it couldn't keep it all together!

Why did the frog bring a backpack to school?

To carry its croak-lator!

What's a pirate's least favorite school subject?

Arrrrrr-tithmetic!

Why did the marker always feel important?

Because it could highlight everything!

What's the principal's favorite dance move?

The rule breaker shuffle!

Why was the student always cold in math class?

Because they couldn't find their degree!

What do you call a notebook that loves to gossip?

A tell-all journal!.

CHAPTER 7. GIGGLES ON THE GO

Why did the car bring a blanket to the garage?

It wanted to take a nap in the car-pet!

What's a bus's favorite kind of music?

Heavy traffic!

Why don't trains ever play hide-and-seek?

Because they always leave tracks!

What's a pilot's favorite snack?

Plane chips!

Why was the boat so good at telling jokes?

It always had the current humor!

Why did the airplane get an award?

Because it was outstanding in its field... of clouds!

What do cars eat on road trips?

Traffic jams!

Why was the tire so bad at basketball?

Because it always bounced too much!

What's a taxi's favorite game?

Pick-up sticks!

Why did the train cross the road?

To get to the other track!

Why don't bicycles ever tell secrets?

Because they have too many spokes-people!

What's an astronaut's favorite mode of transportation?

The space shuttle bus!

Why did the scooter get in trouble?

It was always pushing its luck!

What's a bus driver's favorite vegetable?

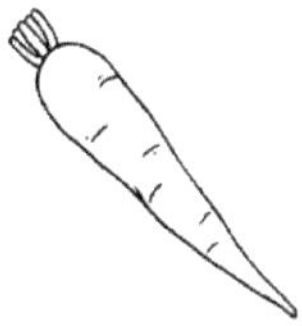

Car-rots!

Why did the helicopter refuse to land?

It was having a high time!

What do you call a car that tells jokes?

A real crack-up truck!

Why did the ferry blush?

Because it saw the buoy!

What do trains do when they get a cold?

They choo-choo sneeze!

What's a suitcase's favorite dessert?

Packing cake!

Why was the bicycle afraid of hills?

It didn't want to go downhill fast!

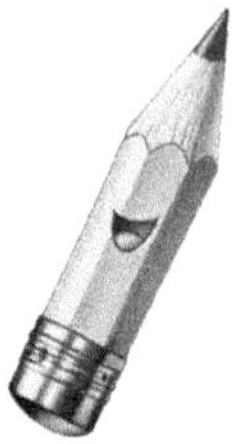

Why did the jet bring a pencil?

To draw its flight path!

What's a bus's favorite vegetable?

A bushel of corn!

Why do boats never forget things?

Because they always have a good anchor point!

What's a car's least favorite kind of joke?

One that's exhausting!

Why did the hot air balloon never argue?

Because it always wanted to stay above things!

Why did the traffic light break up with the car?

It needed space to change!

What's a train's favorite part of a meal?

The tracks of snacks!

Why did the airplane sit down to read?

It wanted to take a literary journey!

What's a taxi's favorite dance?

The fare-well shuffle!

Why did the canoe bring a pillow?

It was ready for a streamy nap!

What do you call a singing airplane?

A soprano jet!

Why do cars never get lonely?

Because they always have good company on the road!

What's a sailboat's favorite candy?

Lifesavers!

Why did the train get promoted?

It was always on the right track!

What do cars like to eat for breakfast?

Oat-wheel cereal!

Why was the road so smart?

Because it had a lot of paved experience!

What's a bird's favorite way to travel?

A feather plane!

Why don't ships ever fight?

Because they don't want to rock the boat!

What's a bus driver's favorite movie?

Speed bumps in action!

Why did the rocket take music lessons?

So it could play in orbit-stras!

Why did the bicycle refuse dessert?

It was already two-tired for more!

What's a car's favorite exercise?

Wheel poses in yoga!

Why do airplanes make bad comedians?

Because their jokes never land!

What do you call a truck that tells spooky stories?

A haul-o-ween truck!

Why did the train love math?

Because it was always calculating its speed!

What's a boat's favorite part of a movie?

The anchor scene!

Why don't bikes like scary movies?

Because they brake easily!

What do you call a car that snores?

A sleepy sedan!

Why did the plane bring a ladder?

To reach new heights!

What's a ship captain's favorite snack?

Sea-salted chips!

What did the van say to the road?

"I'm driving this conversation!"

Why did the train take a nap?

It was feeling derailed!

What's a pilot's favorite math problem?

A plane geometry question!

What do you call a boat full of laughing people?

A giggle ship!

Why did the camper go to art school?

It wanted to learn to draw maps!

What's a bus driver's favorite kind of dog?

A Greyhound!

Why was the ship great at multitasking?

Because it could stay on course and float ideas!

Why don't airplanes ever go on diets?

Because they always wing it!

What did the traffic light say to the car?

"Don't look now, I'm about to change!"

What's a traveler's favorite candy?

Roam-pops!

Why did the boat take a bow?

It was feeling knot-worthy!

Why did the car start writing poetry?

Because it had so many driven emotions!

What do buses wear to stay warm?

Routes!

Why was the airplane so polite?

Because it had great air manners!

What do you call a boat with no crew?

Oar-phaned!

Why don't trains ever get bored?

Because they're always moving forward!

Why did the car's engine love puzzles?

It liked to solve problems under the hood!

What's a jet's favorite fruit?

Blue-sky berries!

Why did the ship always win races?

It had a sailing advantage!

What do you call a bus that tells jokes?

A laugh coach!

Why did the airplane tell a joke?

It wanted to see how far it would fly!

What do you call a snail on a skateboard?

Fast and Sluggish!

Why did the car need glasses?

Because it lost its focus!

What do you call a train that can't stop telling jokes?

A real loco-motive!

Why was the hot air balloon so bad at keeping secrets?

Because it was always letting things slip!

What's a truck's favorite kind of sandwich?

A big rig roast beef!

Why did the GPS go to therapy?

It had trouble finding its direction in life!

What do you call a plane that only tells dad jokes?

A corny-concorde!

Why did the train go to school?

To choo-choo-se a new career path!

What's a ship's least favorite weather?

Pier pressure!

Why did the car get a ticket at the vegetable market?

It couldn't resist parking on the lettuce!

What did one wheel say to the other?

"Stop spinning—I'm getting tired of this!"

Why did the rowboat bring a book?

To stay a-float with knowledge!

Why did the school bus go to music lessons?

It wanted to get better at its horn solo!

Why don't cars ever get into arguments?

Because they always take the high road!

What do you call a really funny motorcycle?

A laughing Harley!

Why did the plane always win at hide-and-seek?

Because no one could spot it!

What's a ship's favorite magic trick?

Disappear-o under the pier-o!

What do you call a car with no wheels?

Grounded!

Why did the cyclist take up gardening?

They wanted to plant some spokes-personality!

Why don't airplanes play baseball?

Because they might strike out too high!

What do buses use to stay organized?

Route maps!

What do you call a boomerang in a car?

Crash and return!

Why do kayaks never tell jokes?

Because they're always paddling out of trouble!

What's a truck's favorite subject in school?

Haul-gebra!

Why did the airplane bring a rope?

In case it needed to tie up loose ends!

What's a train conductor's favorite animal?

A choo-choo-nicorn!

Why don't helicopters ever get lost?

Because they're always hovering over maps!

What did the cruise ship say to the tugboat?

"You really float my boat! "

Why did the GPS start a band?

Because it always knew how to lead the way!

Chapter 8. Tongue Twisters

Chirpy chicks choose chunky chocolate chips cheerfully.

Tiny turtles tiptoed through tulip tunnels ten times today.

Silly Sally's slippery sandals slide on soggy sand.

Bright blue birds boldly bounce between big branches.

Five funny frogs found furry flies in the forest.

Wiggly worms wiggle wildly while weaving through wet weeds.

Ten tall trees towered above twenty tiny toads.

Fizzy fishes flip flopped freely in frothy foam.

Peter's pet parrot picked purple peppers perfectly.

Greedy goats gobble green grapes in Grandpa's garden.

Seven sneaky seals swam swiftly through sparkling seas.

Bobby's bouncy balloon burst before his birthday bash.

Fluffy foxes found fifty fresh figs for a feast.

Kooky kangaroos kicked crunchy coconuts across the canyon.

Zippy zebras zigzagged through zesty zucchini fields.

Merry mice munch melted marshmallows by moonlight.

Lazy lions lounge on leafy logs in long lines.

Gigantic giraffes gently grabbed green gumdrops.

Funky flamingos flap furiously in funny feathered formations.

Cranky crabs carry colorful candy canes to the coast.

Teeny tiny tigers tap tambourines together tirelessly.

Big brown bears balanced boxes of bananas beautifully.

Quick quails quietly quizzed quirky queens about quiche.

Clumsy clowns climbed countless colorful cotton candy cliffs.

Squeaky squirrels stashed shiny silver shells secretly.

Tongue Twisters for Kids (26-50)

Jumpy jellybeans jiggled joyfully in a jumbled jar.

Pink pandas painted polka dots on purple pansies.

Careful caterpillars crawl cautiously carrying crunchy carrots.

Six slippery seals slipped slowly across slick stones.

Bold bunnies baked buttery biscuits for Bella's birthday.

Wobbly walruses waltzed wildly wearing woolly waistcoats.

Chubby chipmunks chomped chocolate chip churros cheerily.

Penny's picky puppy pranced past piles of pancakes.

Round raccoons raced rapidly around Robin's rocking red raft.

Clever clams clapped constantly in Carl's crowded clam cove.

Freddy's fried fish flopped fantastically on his fork.

Nifty newts nibbled on nine navy-blue nectarines.

Spiky spiders spun sparkling silvery spiderwebs swiftly.

Boisterous bees buzzed busily by blooming bluebells.

Frosty foxes followed faint footprints through frozen fields.

Squishy squids squirted super sour seaweed smoothies.

Grumpy geese gobbled gooey green gummy grapes.

Plucky penguins popped pink popcorn in Peter's pantry.

Speedy snails slid sideways down slippery stone steps.

Shiny shoes shined silently under sunny skies.

Tiny terrapins tapped tunes on tin tambourines.

Bouncy bunnies bounced between brightly blooming bushes.

Zany zebras zipped past zooming zippers in zigzags.

Dizzy dogs danced dreamily under dazzling disco lights.

Happy hedgehogs hid heaps of honeydew in hollow logs.

CHAPTER 9. SEASONAL CHUCKLES

Why did the snowman refuse to fight?

Because he didn't want to get into a frosty situation!

What's a turkey's favorite dance move?

The wobble!

Why did the Easter egg hide?

It was a little chicken!

What do you call a beach party in winter?

A cold front flip!

Why did the skeleton refuse to trick-or-treat?

Because it didn't have the guts!

Why are spring flowers so polite?

Because they always bloom where they're planted!

What do you call Santa when he takes a vacation?

Chill Claus!

Why did the leaf break up with the tree?

It found someone with more bark!

What's a snowman's favorite cereal?

Frosted Flakes!

Why do pumpkins sit on porches?

Because they don't have any gourd furniture!

Why don't scarecrows tell secrets?

Because the corn is all ears!

What do reindeer say before telling a joke?

"This one will sleigh you!"

What's a witch's favorite subject in school?

Spelling!

What do trees say when they're surprised?

"That's unbe-leaf-able!"

What do elves learn in school?

The elf-abet!

Why did the sun go to school?

To get a little brighter!

What do you call a summer snowman?

A puddle!

Why do ghosts love parties?

Because they know how to boo-gie!

What's a Christmas tree's least favorite sport?

Boxing!

What did one raindrop say to the other?

"You're making quite a splash!"

Why are snowflakes so bad at keeping secrets?

Because they always flake out!

What do turkeys use to fix their feathers?

Quack tape!

Why do bees stay in their hives during the winter?

They're on buzz-cation!

Seasonal Chuckles (26-50)

What do you call a funny Valentine's card?

Punny love!

Why did the ghost go to the party?

To lift its spirits!

Why do flowers love spring?

Because it's their time to shine!

What's a snowman's favorite dessert?

Ice cream sandwiches!

Why don't skeletons like winter?

They can't handle the chill!

What's a shark's favorite holiday?

Fin-dependence Day!

What do you call a bunny with a bad attitude?

A real hop-head!

What do you call a Halloween cookie?

A boo-scone!

Why do reindeer wear bells?

Because their horns don't jingle!

What's a scarecrow's favorite weather?

Patchy sunshine!

Why was the Christmas tree late?

It got stuck in a pine-up!

What do fireworks eat for breakfast?

Snap, crackle, and pop!

What's a ghost's favorite dessert?

Ice scream!

Why did the turkey go to space?

To prove it wasn't a chicken!

What do you call a snowman that tells jokes?

Pun-derful!

What's the Easter Bunny's favorite type of music?

Hip-hop!

What do you call a friendly pumpkin?

Gourdeous!

Why did the leaf jump off the tree?

It wanted to branch out!

What do witches put on their bagels?

Scare-ream cheese!

What's Santa's favorite type of sandwich?

A ho-ho-hoagie!

Why are turkeys terrible at math?

They always forget to carry the one!

What did the rain cloud say to the sun?

"You're stealing my thunder!

Why do ghosts like snowstorms?

Because it's boo-tiful!

What's a snowman's favorite movie?

Frozen!

What do you call a beach-loving elf?

Sand-a Claus!

Why do eggs love Easter?

Because they get to crack jokes!

What's a summer watermelon's favorite job?

Lifeguard!

Why don't skeletons ever lie?

Because you can see right through them!

What's a Christmas elf's favorite drink?

Hot choc-elf-late!

What do clouds wear under their raincoats?

Thunderwear!

Why did the leaf refuse to play hide and seek?

It didn't want to get raked in!

What's a polar bear's favorite snack?

Brrrr-itos!

Why are bunnies so good at math?

They can multiply hoppily!

What do you call a snowman that loves jokes?

Pun-sicle!

Why did the turkey sit on the cake?

Because it wanted to gobble it up!

What do vampires eat on Thanksgiving?

Grave-y!

What's a witch's favorite holiday game?

Hide and shriek!

Why do snowflakes never argue?

They always fall into place!

What's a pumpkin's favorite sport?

Squash!

What do you call Santa's helpers who love karate?

The Santa Chop Squad!

Why do summer campers tell ghost stories?

Because they love a good s'moral!

What do you call a bunny who tells jokes?

A real hare-larious comedian!

Why don't scarecrows eat snacks?

They're already stuffed!

What's a snowman's favorite type of weather?

Snow way too warm!

Why did the Christmas ornament go to the party?

To have a ball!

What do you call a skeleton who works out?

A bone-afide athlete!

Why do turkeys love puzzles?

They like to piece things together!

What did the summer sun say to the ice cream?

"I'm going to melt your heart!

What do ghosts wear to the beach?

Boo-kinis!

Why did the Easter Bunny buy a new hat?

To look egg-stra fancy!

CHAPTER 10. SUPERHERO & ADVENTURE JOKES

Why did the superhero start a cleaning business?

Because he was great at "sweeping" villains off their feet!

How do superheroes stay in shape?

They do "super" squats!

Why did the villain join a band?

He wanted to be the "lead singer" of evil!

Why did the hero bring a pencil to the fight?

He wanted to "draw" some attention to himself!

What's a superhero's favorite time of day?

"Super" early in the morning!

What did the superhero say when his friend asked for help?

"I'm always here to 'save the day'!"

Why did the sidekick go to the doctor?

He was feeling a little "side" sick!

What do superheroes call their gym?

"The Powerhouse"!

Why did the villain refuse to eat his vegetables?

He couldn't "digest" good plans!

How does a superhero order pizza?

With "super" delivery, of course!

Why don't superheroes ever go to the beach?

They don't want to get "sand"-wich-ed between villains!

What's the superhero's favorite candy?

"Super" gummies!

Why did the villain bring a pencil to the treasure hunt?

To “sketch” out his plans!

What do you call a superhero who’s always forgetting things?

“Memory Man!”

Why did the superhero avoid the computer?

He was afraid of catching a “virus”!

What did the superhero say to the evil scientist?

“You’re really ‘blowing’ things out of proportion!”

Why did the villain refuse to fight at night?

Because he couldn’t “see” the point!

What’s a superhero’s favorite snack?

“Power” bars!

Why did the hero wear a helmet on his mission?

To “head” off any problems!

What do you call a superhero who's great at math?

"Algebraman"!

Why was the superhero always so calm?

Because he had "super" control!

How did the villain plan to escape the island?

With a "plane" of evil escape!

What do you call a superhero who loves puzzles?

"Piece" Man!

Why did the villain fail at cooking?

Because he was always "burning" his plans!

What do superheroes do when they're hungry?

They "super" snack!

Why did the sidekick wear a cape?

To be ready for any "side" action!

What's a superhero's favorite dance move?

The "power slide!"

Why did the villain hate reading?

He couldn't get through the "evil chapters"!

What did the hero say after stopping the robbery?

"That's what you get for trying to 'steal' the show!"

Why did the superhero take a nap during the mission?

He needed some "super" rest before saving the day!

What do superheroes do after a big meal?

They go on a "super" jog!

Why was the villain always talking about cheese?

He was obsessed with making "grate" plans!

What do you call a superhero who is always prepared?

"Plan-man!"

Why did the superhero bring a bucket to the rescue?

To "carry" out his mission!

How does a superhero brush his teeth?

With a "power" toothbrush!

What do you call a superhero who can juggle?

"Multi-task Man!"

Why did the villain refuse to use his superpowers?

Because he was "out of power"!

How do superheroes stay hydrated?

With "super" water, of course!

What do superheroes use to keep their houses clean?

"Super" vacuums!

Why did the hero always wear sunglasses?

To protect his "super" eyes from the spotlight!

What did the villain say after tripping on the stairs?

"I knew this was going to be a 'downward' spiral!"

What's a superhero's favorite type of tree?

A "palm" tree for the ultimate relaxation!

Why did the villain start gardening?

He wanted to "grow" his plans in a more "natural" way!

What do superheroes eat at the movies?

"Super" popcorn!

Why did the villain wear a cape to work?

He thought it would make him "super" productive!

What do superheroes use to fix a car?

"Super" wrenches!

How does a superhero take a break?

With a "super" snack and a super show!

Why did the hero decide to become a chef?

He was great at "flipping" the situation!

How did the villain feel after losing the fight?

"Defeated" but still "bad to the bone"!

What did the superhero do when he was tired of fighting?

He "super" rested before the next mission!

Why did the villain start wearing a mask?

He was "hiding" his true identity!

What's the superhero's favorite subject at school?

"Super" history—because every hero has one!

Why did the superhero make friends with the dragon?

They both had "fire" in their hearts!

What did the hero say to his sidekick when they were out of snacks?

"Looks like we'll have to 'save' lunch for later!"

Why did the superhero use a pencil sharpener?

To keep his "super" ideas sharp!

What do you call a superhero who's also a magician?

"Abra-cadabra Man"!

Why did the villain join a fitness class?

He needed to work on his "bad" posture!

What do superheroes wear at a wedding?

"Super" tuxedos, of course!

CHAPTER 11. FUNNY FACTS

Did you know?

A crocodile can't stick out its tongue!

Guess it's always "biting" its tongue!

Fun fact:

A shrimp's heart is in its head!

That's one "head" over heels shrimp!

Did you hear?

Slugs have four noses!

They're always "sniffing" out new smells!

Fun fact:

A group of owls is called a "parliament"!

Must be the smartest group in the animal kingdom!

Did you know?

Honey never spoils!

So, the next time you find honey in your pantry, it's still "sweet" as ever!

Fun fact:

An octopus has three hearts!

It must really "love" hugging you!

Did you hear?

Elephants are the only animals that can't jump!

But they sure "trumpet" with pride!

Did you know?

A group of flamingos is called a "flamboyance"!

Sounds like they're throwing a "fabulous" party!

Fun fact:

Giraffes have no vocal cords!

They must be really "silent" but tall at the same time!

Did you hear?

A cheetah can run up to 60 miles per hour!

Talk about a "fast" delivery!

Fun fact:

Kangaroos can't walk backward!

They're always "hopping" forward into the future!

Did you know?

A snail can sleep for three years!

I guess it takes "resting" to a whole new level!

Fun fact:

Wombats have cube-shaped poop!

They're the real "block" party animals!

Did you hear?

A blue whale's tongue weighs as much as an elephant!

Talk about having a "heavy" opinion!

Did you know?

Cows have best friends!

They're moo-ving in the friendship department!

Fun fact:

Koalas sleep up to 22 hours a day!

They're "koala-fied" nappers!

Did you know?

Polar bears have black skin under their white fur!

They're "black and white" and ready for winter!

Fun fact:

A group of rhinos is called a "crash"!

Sounds like a "smashing" good time!

Did you hear?

A jellyfish is 95% water!

Talk about being a "fluid" creature!

Did you know?

Ants never sleep!

They're always "ant"-icipating the next adventure!

Fun fact:

Turtles can breathe through their butts!

Guess they're "full of hot air" in more ways than one!

Did you hear?

Some frogs can freeze and still live!

They're "cool" under pressure!

Did you know?

A giraffe's neck is too short to reach the ground!

I guess it's always "looking up" in life!

Fun fact:

Sea otters hold hands while sleeping to keep from drifting apart!

They're all about "otterly" cute teamwork!

Did you know?

Bats are the only mammals that can fly!

They must be "bat"-tastic at flying!

Fun fact:

The shortest war in history was between Britain and Zanzibar in 1896.

It lasted only 38 minutes! Guess they couldn't "war"-ry about it for long!

Did you hear?

A hummingbird's heart can beat 1,200 times per minute!

That's a "heart-thumping" speed!

Did you know?

A honeybee can fly up to 15 miles per hour!

Talk about a "buzzing" speedster!

Fun fact:

Some sharks can live up to 400 years!

They're the "ancient" swimmers of the sea!

Did you know?

The longest hiccuping spree lasted 68 years!

Talk about being "stuck" in the middle of a hiccup!

Fun fact:

Penguins propose to their mates with a pebble!

It's their version of a "rock-solid" relationship!

Did you hear?

There are more stars in the universe than grains of sand on all the Earth's beaches!

That's an "out of this world" fact!

Did you know?

A mole can dig a tunnel 300 feet long in just one night!

It's like a "subterranean" marathon!

Fun fact:

A single cloud can weigh more than a million pounds!

That's a "heavy" thought to float on!

Did you hear?

A shrimp can regrow its heart!

Talk about "hearty" recovery!

Did you know?

A crocodile can't stick out its tongue!

Guess it's a little "tongue-tied"!

Fun fact:

You can't hum while holding your nose!

It's a "nose-tingling" challenge!

Did you hear?

The Eiffel Tower can grow by up to 6 inches in the summer!

It's the "stretching" marvel of Paris!

Did you know?

A snail can travel 0.03 miles per hour!

It's the "slow and steady" racer of the animal kingdom!

Fun fact:

Cheetahs can accelerate from 0 to 60 mph in just a few seconds!

They're the "fast" and furious of the jungle!

Did you hear?

A giraffe's tongue can be up to 18 inches long!

That's one "long" reach for a snack!

Did you know?

A platypus doesn't have a stomach!

I guess it "stomachs" things in a whole new way!

Fun fact:

A group of hedgehogs is called a "prickle"!

They must have "sharp" personalities!

Did you hear?

Some fish can walk on land!

I guess they're "fin-ally" ready to explore!

Did you know?

A cockroach can live for weeks without its head!

It's truly "headstrong"!

Fun fact:

The longest hiccuping spree lasted 68 years!

Now that's a "long time to hold your breath"!

Did you hear?

A starfish can regrow its arms!

It's the "ultimate" in multitasking!

Did you know?

There are over 7,000 languages spoken in the world today!

That's a lot of "words" to juggle!

Fun fact:

Most kangaroos are left-handed!

Guess they prefer "hopping" on the left side of life!

Did you know?

A baby panda weighs about the same as a cup of tea when born!

They're "panda"-monium in the making!

Fun fact:

The longest hiccuping spree lasted 68 years!

That's one "long hiccup" journey!

Did you hear?

A snail can sleep for up to three years!

Talk about "snail-ing" through life!

Did you know?

A group of flamingos is called a "flamboyance"!

It's a party waiting to happen!

Fun fact:

A koala's fingerprint is so similar to a human's that it can be mistaken for one!

A "koala-fied" crime suspect!

Did you know?

Giraffes only sleep about 20 minutes a day!

They're "dreaming big" with very little time!

Fun fact:

An octopus has three hearts and blue blood!

It's the "royalty" of the sea!

Did you hear?

The shortest commercial flight in the world lasts just 57 seconds!

That's a "blink" of an eye!

Did you know?

Polar bear skin is black!

They're "black and white" and ready for the cold!

Fun fact:

Jellyfish are 95% water!

Talk about being a "fluid" creature!

Did you hear?

The first ever computer bug was an actual bug!

It's a "literal" problem in the system!

Did you know?

A cheetah's acceleration can outpace a sports car!

It's the "fastest" in the animal kingdom!

Fun fact:

A butterfly's taste buds are on its feet!

It's always "treading" carefully when choosing snacks!

Did you know?

Dolphins have names for each other!

Talk about a “whale” of a time remembering names!

Did you hear?

A hummingbird’s wings

CHAPTER 12. CREATE YOUR OWN JOKES!

Welcome to the **Create Your Own Jokes** chapter, where you can become a joke master! Have you ever wondered how to make your own jokes that will have everyone laughing? Well, you're in the right place! In this chapter, we're going to teach you how to craft your very own hilarious jokes, just like the ones you've been reading in this book.

What Makes a Joke Funny?

Before we start creating your own jokes, let's talk about what makes a joke funny. All good jokes have two key parts:

1. **The Setup** – This is where you tell a situation or ask a question. The setup builds a little bit of suspense.

2. **The Punchline** – This is where you surprise your audience! The punchline gives the funny twist or answer to the setup.

A joke works best when the punchline is unexpected but makes sense! Let's see how it works.

Example:

Setup: Why did the computer go to the doctor?
Punchline: Because it had a virus!

The setup makes you think the computer might be sick, and the punchline surprises you by giving a funny twist – the computer has a "virus" like a human might!

How to Create Your Own Jokes

Now that you understand the basics, let's dive into how to create your own fun jokes! Don't worry, it's easier than you think, and all you need is a little creativity.

Step 1: Choose a Fun Topic

Think about things that make you laugh! Here are some ideas to help you get started:

- **Animals** – Animals are always funny! Think about their habits, sounds, or what they might do if they could talk.
- **School** – What's funny about school? Teachers, homework, recess, or even lunch can be great topics.
- **Food** – What happens when you talk about your favorite food? There are plenty of funny situations to explore!
- **Friends and Family** – Sometimes, the silly things your friends and family do can be perfect for a joke.
- **Superheroes and Adventures** – Who wouldn't laugh at a superhero doing something totally unexpected?

Step 2: Create a Setup

Your setup can be a question or a funny situation. Here are some ideas:

- **Question Jokes**: Start with "Why," "What," or "How."
    - **Example**: Why did the cat sit on the computer?
- **Situation Jokes**: Start with a funny scene or idea.
    - **Example**: I walked into the kitchen and found a chicken trying to use the microwave!

Step 3: Add a Surprising Punchline

Now, think of a funny twist or answer for your setup. The punchline should surprise the listener but still make sense with the setup.

Here are some punchline ideas to help:

- Play with words that sound the same but have different meanings (called **puns**).
- Think about what's unexpected. If your setup says one thing, your punchline could do the opposite.
- Use silly logic, like imagining something impossible or funny about everyday situations.

Example Punchlines:

- For the cat and computer joke:
  Punchline: Because it wanted to keep an eye on the mouse!
- For the chicken and microwave joke:
  Punchline: It was trying to "cook" up some ideas!

Step 4: Write Your Joke!

Now it's time to put your setup and punchline together. Here's how a joke looks:

Setup: Why did the giraffe bring a ladder to the party?
Punchline: Because it wanted to reach new heights of fun!

You did it! Now you have your own original joke!

Practice Makes Perfect

You can keep practicing by coming up with more setups and punchlines. It might take a few tries to find the perfect combination, and that's okay! Some jokes might make you giggle, and some might need a little tweaking. That's all part of the fun.

Joke Writing Exercises

Here are some fun exercises to get your imagination flowing:

1. **Fill in the blanks**:
    - Why did the ___________ go to the _________?
    - Because it wanted to ___________!
2. **Finish the joke**:
    - What do you call a bear with no teeth?
    - ___________!
3. **Create a twist**:
    - Take a famous saying or phrase and change it to make it funny!
    - Example: "Don't cry over spilled milk" becomes "Don't cry over spilled ice cream!"

Share Your Jokes

Once you've created your jokes, share them with your family and friends! You can even make a mini comedy show. Tell everyone your funniest jokes and watch their faces light up with laughter. They might even ask for more!

Tips for Becoming a Joke Writing Pro:

- **Be silly!** The silliest ideas often make the funniest jokes.

- **Try wordplay**: Playing with words, like puns or rhymes, makes your jokes extra fun.
- **Ask questions**: Kids love jokes that start with "Why" or "How" – they're curious, and it builds excitement.
- **Keep practicing**: The more jokes you write, the better you'll get at it.

Fun Joke Templates for You to Use:

1. **Why did the __________ go to __________?**
   (Fill in the blanks with funny ideas!)
2. **What do you call a __________ that can __________?**
   (Try putting a funny twist on this one!)
3. **If __________ could talk, it would say __________.**
   (Get creative with animal or inanimate objects!)
4. **How do you make a __________ laugh?**
   (Think of funny things that could make an object or person laugh!)

Congratulations! You're a Joke Writer Now!

We hope you have lots of fun creating your own jokes. Remember, there's no limit to the fun you can have with your imagination. So go ahead—write some jokes, share them with your friends and family, and watch everyone laugh. Who knows? You might even become the funniest person in your school or family!

Happy joke-making!

CHAPTER 13. BONUS LAUGHS

Why did the bicycle fall over?

Because it was two-tired!

What do you call an alligator in a vest?

An in-vest-igator!

Why did the cow go to space?

To see the moooon!

What's a skeleton's least favorite room?

The living room!

What do you get when you cross a snowman with a vampire?

Frostbite!

Why did the student bring a ladder to school?

Because he wanted to go to high school!

What's orange and sounds like a parrot?

A carrot!

Why did the pencil go to the party?

Because it wanted to draw attention!

What do you call a bear with no teeth?

A gummy bear!

Why can't you trust an atom?

Because they make up everything!

Why do cows wear bells?

Because their horns don't work!

What's a vampire's favorite fruit?

A blood orange!

What do you call a pile of kittens?

A meow-tain!

Why don't eggs tell jokes?

They might crack up!

Why do fish always know how much they weigh?

Because they have scales!

Why did the tomato turn red?

Because it saw the salad dressing!

What do you call a fake noodle?

An impasta!

Why don't skeletons fight each other?

They don't have the guts!

What did the ocean say to the beach?

Nothing, it just waved!

Why don't skeletons ever use cell phones?

Because they don't have thumbs!

What do you call a bear who loves to surf?

A grizzly wave rider!

Why was the broom late?

It swept in!

What do you call a sleeping bull?

A bulldozer!

Why did the bicycle refuse to race?

It was two-tired!

What's a dog's favorite instrument?

The barkphone!

Why did the snowman want a suntan?

Because he was feeling a little chilly!

What do you call a snail on a ship?

A snailor!

Why did the duck get a job?

To get some quackers!

Why do bees have sticky hair?

Because they use honeycombs!

What's a skeleton's favorite instrument?

The trom-bone!

Why did the mushroom go to the party?

Because he was a fun-gi!

What do you call a bear with a bad attitude?

A grizzly bear!

What do cows like to do at night?

Go to moo-vies!

Why did the bicycle go to the gym?

It wanted to get two-tired!

What do you get when you cross a dog with a computer?

A lot of byte!

Why don't skeletons ever tell secrets?

Because they don't have any skin!

What do you call a group of unorganized cats?

A cat-astrophe!

Why did the dragon sleep all day?

It was dragon its feet!

What do you call a fish with no eyes?

A fsh!

Why do giraffes have long necks?

Because their heads are so far away!

Why don't spiders use computers?

Because they're afraid of getting webbed!

Why did the carrot get an award?

Because it was out-standing in its field!

What's a vampire's favorite kind of dog?

A bloodhound!

Why was the broom always tired?

Because it swept all night!

What do you get when you cross a snowman with a dog?

Frostbite!

Why do cows love to read?

Because they're always moo-ved by books!

What did the ocean say to the sand?

Nothing, it just waved!

Why don't eggs tell secrets?

Because they might crack up!

What's a skeleton's favorite type of pizza?

Bones-apart!

Why did the dog sit in the shade?

Because it didn't want to be a hot dog!

What did one plate say to the other plate?

Lunch is on me!

Why did the mushroom go to the party?

Because he was a fungi!

What did the grape say when it got stepped on?

Nothing, it just let out a little wine!

Why don't skeletons ever fight each other?

They don't have the stomach for it!

Why was the dog sitting at the computer?

To log in!

What did the bee say to the flower?

Hey, bud, what's up?!

What's a ghost's favorite dessert?

Boo-berries!

Why did the bicycle fall over?

It was two-tired!

Why don't skeletons like to party?

They don't have the bones to dance!

What did one pencil say to the other pencil?

You're looking sharp!

Why don't lions ever tell secrets?

Because they don't want to li-on!

What did the ocean say to the wave?

Nothing, it just waved!

Why was the music teacher always so good at solving problems?

Because she was always in tune with the issues!

Why did the dog bring a pencil to school?

Because it wanted to be a ruff writer!

What did one snowman say to the other snowman?

Do you smell carrots?!

What's a cat's favorite color?

Purr-ple!

Why did the bicycle have a flat tire?

Because it was two-tired!

What do you get when you cross a kangaroo and a snake?

A jump rope!

Why did the grape stop in the middle of the road?

Because it ran out of juice!

What do you get when you cross an elephant and a rhinoceros?

Elephino (I'll-effin-o)!

Why don't elephants make good dancers?

Because they have two left feet!

Why did the dog sit under the tree?

Because it was a barking up the wrong tree!

Why did the cat wear a fancy dress?

Because she was going to a purr-ty!

What's a dog's favorite type of pizza?

Paw-peroni!

Why don't fish ever play basketball?

Because they're afraid of the net!

Why was the math book so unhappy?

Because it had too many problems!

Why don't sharks like fast food?

Because they can't catch it!

What's a dog's favorite city?

New York!

Why did the chicken join the band?

Because it had the drumsticks!

What did the duck say when he bought a lipstick?

Put it on my bill!

Why can't you ever trust a pencil?

Because it's always pointing fingers!

What do you get when you cross a snowman with a vampire?

Frostbite!

Why don't skeletons like to party?

They don't have the stomach for it!

What did one hat say to the other hat?

Stay here, I'm going on ahead!

Why did the cow go to outer space?

To see the moon!

Why do cows wear bells?

Because their horns don't work!

CHAPTER 14. FINAL GIGGLE ROUND

Why did the scarecrow win an award?

Because he was outstanding in his field!

What did one plate say to the other plate?

Lunch is on me!

Why don't skeletons fight?

They don't have the guts!

Why did the teddy bear skip dessert?

Because it was already stuffed!

Knock, knock!

Who's there?

Lettuce.

Lettuce who?

Lettuce in, it's freezing out here!

Why did the math book look so sad?

Because it had too many problems!

What's a cat's favorite color?

Purr-ple!

What do you call a boomerang that doesn't come back?

A stick!

Why can't your nose be 12 inches long?

Because then it would be a foot!

What did the ocean say to the beach?

Nothing, it just waved!

Why don't eggs ever tell jokes?

Because they might crack up!

What do you call a pig that does karate?

A pork chop!

Knock, knock!

Who's there?

Cow says.

Cow says who?

No silly, cow says mooo!

Why did the cookie go to the doctor?

Because it felt crumby!

What kind of tree fits in your hand?

A palm tree!

Why don't dinosaurs ever give high fives?

Because they're all extinct!

What do you call an alligator in a vest?

An investigator!

Why did the banana go to the doctor?

Because it wasn't peeling well!

What's a skeleton's favorite snack?

Spare ribs!

Why did the clock get in trouble at school?

Because it was ticking everyone off!

What's a superhero's favorite part of the joke?

The punchline!

Knock, knock!

Who's there?

Boo.

Boo who?

Don't cry, it's just a joke!

What's a ghost's favorite dessert?

Ice scream!

Why did the tomato blush?

Because it saw the salad dressing!

What kind of shoes do ninjas wear?

Sneakers!

Why did the golfer bring two pairs of pants?

In case he got a hole in one!

What's brown, sticky, and hard to get rid of?

A stick!

What do you call cheese that isn't yours?

Nacho cheese!

Why did thc pony get sent home from school?

Because it had a little horse-play!

Why can't you play hide-and-seek with mountains?

Because they always peak!

What did the frog say when it missed the bus?

Hop on without me!

Why don't spiders get stuck on their own webs?

They know the trick-y parts!

What do astronauts say to their sandwiches?

Launch time!

Knock, knock!

Who's there?

Orange.

Orange who?

Orange you glad this joke is almost over?

Why did the chicken go to the seance?

To get to the other side!

What do you get when you cross a vampire and a snowman?

Frostbite!

Why can't pirates ever learn the alphabet?

Because they always get stuck at R!

Why did the cat sit on the computer?

To keep an eye on the mouse!

What's a ghost's favorite fruit?

Boo-berries!

What do you call a belt with a watch on it?

A waist of time!

Why was the broom late?

It swept in!

What do clouds wear under their clothes?

Thunderwear!

Why was the picture so good at math?

It had a lot of frame work!

What do you call a parade of rabbits hopping backward?

A receding hare-line!

Why did the bird join the band?

Because it had the right tweet!

What did the grape do when it got stepped on?

It let out a little whine!

Why do cows love telling jokes?

Because they're so moo-sing!

What's a kangaroo's favorite drink?

Hop chocolate!

Knock, knock!

Who's there?

Harry.

Harry who?

Harry up, I'm freezing out here!

Why do ducks always pay with cash?

Because they don't like to use bills!

What's a pirate's favorite workout?

The plank!

Why did the astronaut break up with the star?

It needed some space!

Why can't you ever trust stairs?

They're always up to something!

What's a tree's least favorite month?

Sep-timber!

What do you call a sleeping dinosaur?

A dino-snore!

Why don't unicorns play cards?

Because they're afraid of getting decked!

Why did the skeleton go to the barbecue?

To get another rib!

What's a witch's favorite subject?

Spelling!

Why don't sharks play the piano?

Because they can't find the right keys!

What's a magician's favorite candy?

Trick or treats!

Why did the owl get a promotion?

Because it was owl-standing!

Why did the donut visit the dentist?

It needed a filling!

Why did the orange stop halfway through the race?

It ran out of juice!

What did one snowflake say to the other?

You're one of a kind!

What did the spaghetti say to the meatball?

Pasta la vista, baby!

Why do bees always hum?

Because they don't know the words!

Why did the snail refuse to race?

Because it didn't want to come out of its shell!

What do you get if you cross a cow and a trampoline?

A milkshake!

CHAPTER 15. ACKNOWLEDGMENTS AND SPECIAL THANKS

Creating this joke book for kids has been an incredible journey, one filled with laughter, learning, and love. I am overwhelmed with gratitude for the many people who have supported me along the way, and this section is my chance to say a heartfelt thank you to each of you.

First and foremost, to my family: thank you for being my foundation and my greatest cheerleaders. To my husband, who has been my rock through every step of this journey—your unwavering support, encouragement, and belief in me have meant more than words can ever express. You've been my sounding board, my editor, and my partner in everything. Without you, this book would not have been possible.

To my children, and the children in my life, thank you for filling my days with joy, laughter, and endless inspiration. Your giggles and the way you find humor in the simplest moments remind me of the beauty of childhood. You've taught me what it means to see the world through the eyes of a child, and this book is as much for you as it is inspired by you.

To the readers and buyers of this book: thank you for choosing to bring a little extra laughter into your homes and lives. I hope these jokes bring endless smiles to your children, families, and friends. Knowing that my words might bring joy to someone's day is the greatest gift I could ask for.

A special thank-you to school teachers and librarians, who work tirelessly to foster creativity, curiosity, and a love of reading in children. You are the unsung heroes who nurture young minds and inspire future generations. Your dedication to children's growth and imagination is truly remarkable, and I am forever grateful for the magic you bring into their lives.

Finally, to everyone who believes in the power of laughter—thank you for reminding me of its importance. Laughter is universal; it connects us, heals us, and brings light to our lives. I hope this book spreads smiles far and wide, creating moments of joy and togetherness for all who read it.

From the bottom of my heart, thank you. Let's keep sharing laughter, one joke at a time.

ABOUT THE AUTHOR

Mrs. Payel Chakravarty is a passionate writer who blends her technical background with a boundless love for creativity and laughter. Holding a B.Tech and M.Tech in Information Technology, she channels her analytical mind into crafting books that inspire, entertain, and connect with readers of all ages. Based in India, she juggles her roles as a devoted mother of two, author, blogger, ghostwriter, and influencer—all while staying deeply rooted in her spiritual and imaginative side. With *Laughs Unlimited: The Big Book of Jokes for Kids*, Payel continues her mission to spread joy, positivity, and endless smiles through the magic of words.

You can find my website and YouTube channel here:

https://spizevilla.com/

Note: If this book inspires YOU, and enhances your life in any way, it would be a dream come true to see your honest review on Amazon.

www.ingramcontent.com/pod-product-compliance
Ingram Content Group UK Ltd.
Pitfield, Milton Keynes, MK11 3LW, UK
UKHW021344190726
13845UKWH00027B/711

9 789334 301601